Daddy's At Sea

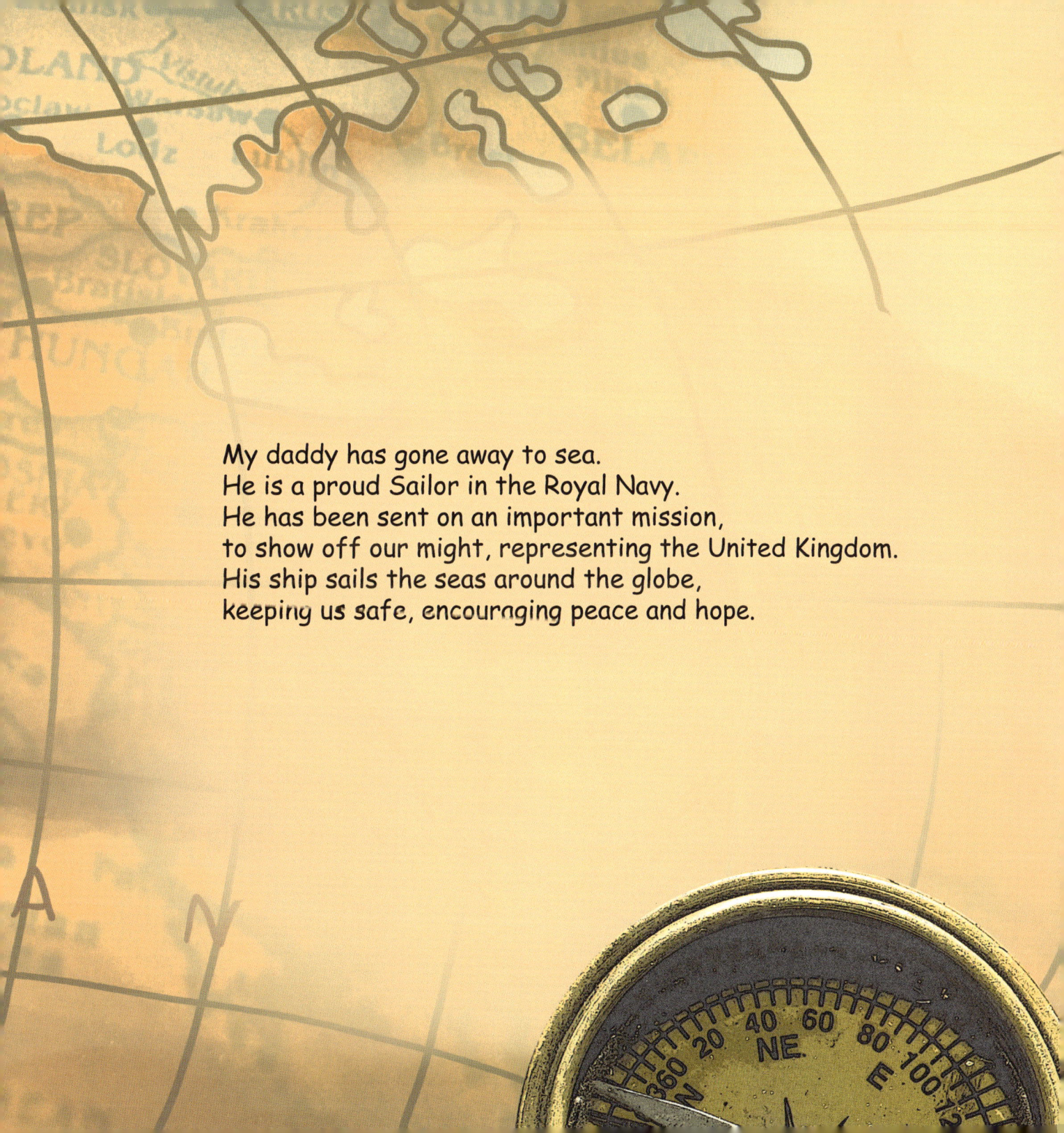

My daddy has gone away to sea.
He is a proud Sailor in the Royal Navy.
He has been sent on an important mission,
to show off our might, representing the United Kingdom.
His ship sails the seas around the globe,
keeping us safe, encouraging peace and hope.

He battles the bad guys, such as smugglers and pirates.
He's a real-life hero, one of the bravest.
But there's no need to worry, the ship is safe.
It's made from metal, it's ginormous, so please keep faith.
Daddy will return safe and sound before long,
exhausted but happy, at home, where he belongs.

Daddy saves people from natural disasters and events,
like hurricanes, earthquakes, and tidal waves to prevent
people from struggling and suffering the impact
of no clean water, no food, or no shelter left intact.
It's humanitarian assistance the Royal Navy provides,
working in challenging conditions with a great sense of pride.

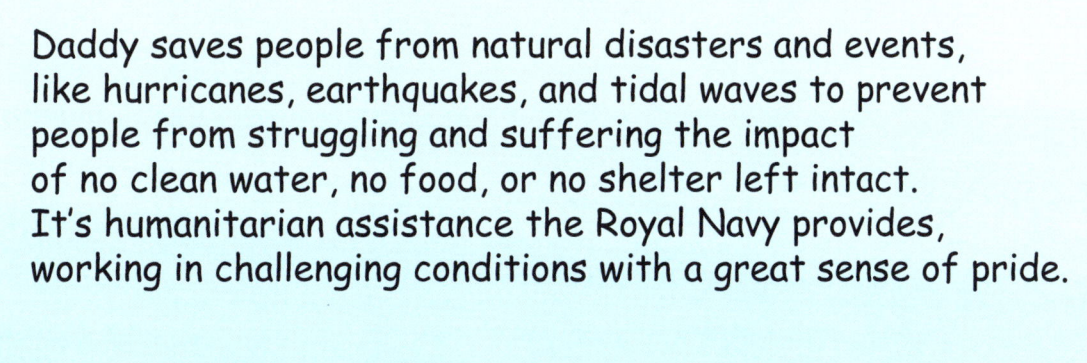

cargo ship

Over British and international waters, Daddy's ship keeps a watchful eye,
to keep Britain's trade goods safe – that's the things Britain buys.
Like cars, toys, TVs, and computers,
mobile phones, gadgets, and even electric scooters!
They're transported to Britain by cargo ship,
and thanks to Daddy, they have a safe trip.

My daddy's a hero, he helps World peace,
by supporting his ship's presence, getting conflict to cease.
His ship proudly sails with a mighty show of force,
letting other countries know, it's peace we endorse.
He keeps the sea safe from criminals and
protects the freedom
of every single person in the United Kingdom.

There's no need to worry about Daddy getting lonely,
he's got friends on the ship and his cabin is quite homely.
With photos of me and our whole family on his wall,
he lays in his bed at night and thinks of us all.
He eats his meals in the mess, the portions are quite hearty.
There's even opportunities for the occasional onboard party.

Mum sometimes gets sad, doing everything alone is a struggle,
but I help her with chores and give lots of cuddles.
Mum misses Daddy but has friends who understand.
They're navy families too and are around to lend a hand.
There are other children in the same boat as me.
They miss their daddy too, because they are at sea.

I find it so hard when Daddy's away.
I miss him so much and count the days.
Mum has a wall chart for me to use.
I tick off each day as it passes, imagining Dad's route,
sailing far and wide across the high seas,
achieving his mission, then homeward bound to me.

I have a sweet jar and each sweet represents
each day Daddy is away from the day he first went.
Every day I take one sweet enjoying its yummy taste.
But for me, it's much sweeter because it's another day faced.
When the day comes that the sweet jar is empty,
I know Daddy's coming home, there'll be celebrations aplenty.

Although I miss Daddy, each day he's gone is tough.
Just like my daddy, I'm brave when the sea is rough.
It's ok to feel sad and I often have a little cry,
thinking of the day we said goodbye.
But one thing's for sure, I'm proud as can be,
to have a daddy who's a sailor in the Royal Navy.

Talula Grey

Talula Grey is a Royal Navy wife, business owner, and writer, but first and foremost, she is a mummy to her young son, a dog, a cat, and some fish. Talula has been married to her sailor husband for 7 years and enjoys the navy life; the lows are challenging, but they make the highs so much more exciting.

Printed in Great Britain
by Amazon

38906780R00016